Criminal Ps

Understanding the Criminal Mind and Its Nature Through Criminal Profiling

ROBERT FORBES

Table of contents

Introduction

I want to thank you and congratulate you for downloading the book, *Criminal Psychology*.

This book contains proven steps and strategies on how to understand what is going on inside the head of serial killers, violent offenders, and the criminals that we see when we look around ourselves.

It is an unnerving thought to realize that anyone could be a violent offender. The potential of the human mind far outreaches anything you could possibly imagine, and to think that they are out and about among us makes it that much more terrifying.

Having an understanding of what goes on inside the mind of a criminal is essential for anything you are doing in regards to criminal studies. Whether you are in school, training to get on with the police force, or just want to further your understanding of what they are thinking and why they do what they do, you have come to the right place.

This book is filled with the ins and outs of criminal psychology as you will see. You will understand why they are the way they are, what causes them to snap, and what you can do to stop this cycle.

Get ready to get a glimpse inside the horrific mind of a killer. Learn what it's like to think as they think and to see as they see. This book is going to take you to the very brink in the mind of a killer, and fill you with the knowledge of what they see and do.

Thanks again for downloading this book, I hope you enjoy it!

Chapter 1 – A Glimpse Inside

We all love that action film. The one with all of the bad guys and the good guys. The good guys always win, of course, because the bad guys... as sinister as they are... are unable to keep up with the intellect of the good guys.

Hollywood and the film industry as a whole has done a great job of painting in our minds the image that criminals and villains are bumbling and idiotic, whereas the policemen and the detectives have it all figured out. It looks as though the criminals are unable to hit a single target they're aiming at, and the police never miss.

The world that is created on screen is a world of safety. One in which even when bad things happen, there's going to be a good guy that can stop it simply because he is "good" and the other guy is "bad".

There is a definitive difference in these movies that real live doesn't have. When you see the villains in these films, they are more often than not clumsy and not sure what is going on.

In real life, serial killers are calculated. It is rare to find one that isn't smart in the realm of how to commit the crime

In real life, spotting a killer may not be so cut and dry, and the actions to follow may not be so black and white. They don't really live in large towers with bright lights at the top, announcing their killings to the world. They don't really have mechanical eyes or black gloves pulled all the way up and over their arms.

They really do look completely normal. They hold normal jobs, they have a wife and a kids, they have friend. They go to the movies, the bars, the grocery store. They have parties and go to parties. They celebrate Christmas and Halloween and Thanksgiving.

From the outside, a serial killer isn't going to stand out like a sore thumb. They look and appear to act just like the rest of society. It's not what's on the outside that is going to tip you off about a serial killer, it's what's on the inside.

While many of them have learning disabilities, you won't find many of them that aren't good at getting away with what they do. They know how to make things happen, and not get caught. If you really think about it, for every serial killer that you do see come to justice, there are countless more that seem to just disappear.

You need to shake out of your mind the villains that you normally see on the television, and start to view them more as the Hannibal the Cannibal character. These are people that known what they are doing. They are real, and what they are doing is real.

The one truth that is ignored in these films, and largely in society as a whole, is the fact that criminals can be very violent people. They aren't the people you see on screen that hold back for one reason or another. More often than not, they take what they want by force, and don't care who gets hurt in the process.

This includes families, women, and children. Sometimes, these three groups are the primary target of the criminal. Other times, they aren't, but they are hurt nonetheless.

Bottom line: violence plays a very big role in society today. Don't believe me? Turn on the news and watch it for 5 minutes. Odds are, you are going to hear about some story that has violence as the baseline. Whether it be a shooting in this place, a beating in that place, or a robbery in another, you just can't get away from it.

Violent people roam the streets, with the complete freedom to act any time they wish.

The question is: where did these violent people come from?

Were they raised differently than those that grew up to be peaceful?

Are there genetics that come into play that cause them to be violent when others aren't?

Do they have a mentality that encourages violence? And if so, why?

Countless questions rise to the surface if you give this any thought at all. After all, criminals are people. They are raised in the same society that each of us are, and they grow up at the same rate. They have the same opportunity to get an honest job and make an honest living as the rest of us do, yet they choose to commit crimes instead.

The question is... why?

What really goes on inside the mind of a serial killer?

What is it that causes them to do what they do, and to do it without thinking twice?

There has to be something that makes them think the way they do. There has to be something that makes them snap.

It's encouraging to know that we have the answers to these questions, but on the other hand it's scary to take note of how little we do know. Over the years, very few serial killers were executed on the spot. Many of them were taken into custody and questioned over and over. Some of them were even released again because of the lack of evidence that could be pinned on them.

They criminals that have been interviewed have been able to provide us with a lot of insight into how they work. Some have given advice to police to help them catch others, some have offered a glimpse into the method behind the madness, but others were completely defiant, and refused to say anything besides they themselves being the victim in the situation.

Using this valuable information and combining it with what we know about the function of the human brain, we are going to explore the reasons these people are the way they are, and what you personally can to do counteract what they are doing.

The key to understanding someone or something is to know exactly why they are doing it, or why it is happening, and that is exactly what you are going to see later on in this book. Let me warn you, some of the examples in this book are graphic, and all of the situations that they partook in are disturbing.

We hope to one day be able to look at the signs and see the patterns in another person's life, and by seeing those patterns to hopefully then turn the person around before it's too late, and we have another serial killer on the prowl.

We are going to get into the actual mind of serial killers and violent offenders, and learn how their brains are functioning, how they are responding, and whether or not they care about what they are doing to other people. With any luck, this book is going to help you understand them, and use this information to dig further into their minds.

After all, there is a reason for why they are behaving this way, isn't there?

Oh there is. And much, much more. In the chapters to come, we are going to learn just what it is that goes on in the mind of a serial killer, and what causes them to kill... and kill again.

Chapter 2 – Some of These Things are Just Like the Others

Before we dive into the subject of how the serial killer's mind works, I want to take a moment to discuss the things they have done, what makes these people fall into the serial killer category, and the things they all have in common.

The vision of a serial killer is often a man that just kills for the fun of it. We think of him going out, catching people, and shooting them or doing something else horrible to them that is quick and painless. We then think of him doing something horrible and obvious with the body to get rid of it, then selecting another victim to begin again.

Through the years, however, there have been certain factors and patterns that come into the lives of each and every serial killer that's on file. What we don't know is if these events are what caused them to be serial killers, or at the very least played a part, or if they are things that happen because they are serial killers.

Here's a brief list of what they have in common, plus a brief overview of each point.

All the serial killers on file have grown up in a broken home in one way or another

We see a pattern in the growing up life of serial killers. They all come from a broken home situation, and later their crimes tend to reveal the brokenness of their home life.

To make it more specific, serial killers tend to have endured some kind of abuse, more often than not sexual in some way, but verbal or physical may also have been present. They're parents were engaging in some sort of bad behavior that brought more distress into their lives, such as alcoholism, drug abuse, physical abuse, or inability to get along with each other.

Some of them saw their parents split up or cheat on each other, some of them were sent from home to live with relatives. The bottom line is they didn't feel accepted or loved during their growing up lives.

All the serial killers on file displayed forms of violence in their childhood or teenage years in one way or another

Sometimes this violence took place when they were as young as 5 or 6 years old, sometimes it didn't show up until they were in their late teens. In some occasions, there are serial killers that have gone to prison as teenagers and were expunged and released when they turned 18 because their crimes took place when they were a minor.

Some of these violent crimes were against other children, other times they were against their parents or other relatives. There is a serial killer that killed both of his grandparents when he was 16, and there is another that murdered a classmate at 13.

Many of them were bullies, and would torture the kids that were much younger than they. They may actually physically abuse them, or they may have just been a standard bully, but the fact is they got pleasure out of torturing the younger children.

Then, there were those that didn't show any violence toward people as kids, but they would do horrible things to animals. The suspicion we have about this is because animals are easy to prey upon. They can't get away, they don't talk back, and not many people are going to step in and stop it.

They would do anything from torture the animal to kill it and mutilate it. Some would torture and animal and bury them, then dig them up again (still living) and continue to torture them. They may have disassembled the body of the animal and tried to reassemble it again later on, or they may have just left it as it was.

The point is there is a definite pattern behind each of these killers, and that pattern started early on.

All the serial killers on file engage in infidelity to their partners

Sexual addiction is another key thing that runs through all of the serial killers on file. Some of them were unfaithful to their spouses through the use of prostitutes or random people they met on the street, others had actual affairs that lasted for great lengths of time.

Many of them would engage in sexual acts with people they intended to murder before they killed them, but there were some that would just have intercourse with the people that fit the profile of their victims, then let them go.

In some situations, the spouse would learn of the infidelity and divorce the killer or they would leave them, but more often than not they had no idea of what was going on until after the killer is arrested and tells all of the details to the police.

All the serial killers sexually abuse their victims (or some of their victims) in some way

Sexual abuse is very common between the killer and the victim. What isn't so common, however, is the method the killer used. For a lot of serial killers, prostitutes were their most common prey, so luring them into a quiet and secluded area was no problem.

They would act like they were going to sleep with the prostitute and pay them like any other client would, but then they would murder the prostitute.

But there were killers who also targeted other people that weren't prostitutes, and the sexual abuse was still a factor. You see a lot of the victims getting drugged and unable to fight back before the killer takes advantage of them, or you see them bound hands and feet before the killer takes advantage.

It is interesting to note on the sidelines, however, that very few of these victims were at the scene with pure intentions. A lot of them were there because these killers told them they were going to take nude photos of them for money, and they agreed, or that they would drink and party before the person left in the morning.

Of course none of these people expected they were going to get murdered in the process, but it is a rare thing when the killer just takes someone off the street by force.

What makes this all take a sick turn is when you realize that serial killers don't just abuse their victims when they are alive. There is a very high number of victims that have been abused after they have been murdered. Many of the killers state that after they murder their victims (usually by strangulation) they would then bury the bodies of the victims somewhere nearby.

Then, after a few days, they would go back and dig the bodies of the victims back up and sexually abuse them again. Now, some of the serial killers greatly enjoyed this and would photograph everything. Others, on the other hand, would be horrified at themselves for this part of their crime and would dismember the bodies and scatter the parts everywhere in an effort to prevent themselves from coming back and doing this again.

All of the serial killers on file did something further to the bodies of their victims after they victim had died

Sexual abuse wasn't enough for the usual serial killer. They would also take apart the bodies and do something with what they had. Some of the serial killers would take body parts from their victims and scatter the pieces all over the state, and at times in multiple states.

Others would preserve different parts of the victim in jars and other preserving fluids. Decapitation is a very common practice for a serial killer, and keeping the skull or trying to preserve the skull of the victim follows shortly after.

Few of the killers actually turned to the cannibalizing of their victims. They would use them in various ways, and one is even noted as trying to serve pieces of her victim to her own children... an act that is blood chillingly close to things the fictional Hannibal Lecter would do.

They would all show great precision in what they did to the bodies, using tools that were almost of surgical grade and meticulously cutting their victims to best preserve the parts. Police would find collections in different parts of their houses or apartments, and on the rare occasion the killer was caught because of the smell that was coming from their home.

All of the serial killers on file opened up to the police at some point in time and gave the authorities more details on killings they had done in the past, as well as pointed out to them where they could find bodies, and further crimes the police didn't know about

While there are some killers that were very open about what they did from the beginning, and there were other killers that hid what they did and denied it even after their arrest, after questioning the killers all admitted their guilt.

None of the killers showed any remorse for the things they had done, and all of them were very graphic in the details of how their victims acted during the process. They would tell the police where they had hidden the bodies, they would mention more victims that the police hadn't known about (and in some instances, couldn't prove that the killer had actually murdered them), and they would show the police where and how they would commit their crimes.

For many, the delivery of the news was cold and calm. They didn't show any signs that they had regretted what they had done to the people, but rather showed regret that they couldn't do a better job in preserving the body parts. There were some that tried to claim insanity (although all of them have been found to be sane at the time of their crimes) and there were some that claimed they were the ones that were the victims of the situation.

As you can see from this list, there are many things serial killers have in common, and as scary as it is, there are a lot of things we can see happening early on in a person's life that could indicate they are on this same path.

What we are trying to do is figure out a way to see the signs and change the outcome, but the problem so far has been that these killers are smart, and they know how to hide what they have done so we don't even know they are the ones committing the crimes for months or even years.

Chapter 3 – Is Discipline the Issue?

If you take a look at the very first point I made on serial killers and the common thread that binds them, you will notice that I said they all come from a broken family in one way or another. Some would take this to mean that they were beaten, abused, or harmed in a way that made them retaliate against life in general.

Other people assume that these serial killers as kids were left alone to do whatever they want. As though they were allowed to do whatever and whenever and that is the reason they are now a grown criminal. They are used to the fact they can get and take and do whatever they want, so they now do it to the extreme of killing other people.

I hate to be the one to have to say it, but discipline isn't necessarily a cut and dry factor in how a child is going to turn out. Yes, a lot of these kids were given the extreme of abuse as children, but certainly not all of them. There were several who were taken out of their abusive homes or taken away from an abusive parent and grew up under the love and guidance of someone that loved them.

They were cared for, sent to school, and taught right and wrong just as any child is. But, there was something deeper going on. Something that was further down than the reach of standard discipline can get to.

There was and is an issue at the heart of the matter. This goes deeper than sending a child to their room or taking away TV for the weekend

We all have our own opinions on how kids ought to be raised. For as many different kinds of parents there are in the world, there are that many different ways of raising kids. Many of them are doing their best, many of them are doing everything they know how to do.

If you were to ask a normal parent how they felt about their child, they would tell you they love their child beyond all measure. There isn't a thing they wouldn't do for their kid, and everything they are doing is to hopefully give their child the chance in life they want them to have.

With that said, there are a number of different ways parents try to teach their kids the difference between right and wrong. For most of us, the general sense of what you should and shouldn't do is born into you, but the other things... all of the moral issues like lying and cheating and stealing... those are the things we are taught not to do early on in life.

But the way those lessons are taught is different from parent to parent.

How to raise children with moral integrity

Moral integrity is a dying trait in today's world. Honesty, kindness, truthfulness, among other things are dying out in a world where selfishness reigns supreme.

But there has to be a way to battle it.

You may have noticed the trend in children's media today to present a problem for the characters, and have the main character solve it through some moral choice. The thought process behind this is that the children will see this behavior modeled in the shows they like, and the outcome will be good for the character.

With that in mind, they will, in turn, make the same kind of moral decisions in life.

Sadly, this isn't enough. If we are going to step in and make an actual difference in a child's life, there has got to be a lot more involvement there than just setting them in front of a television show and hoping they will pick up on the moral traits of the characters.

There are definite steps that can be taken that will make a major difference in the moral outcome for our children. Some methods are definitely more effective than others, but let's take a look at all of them and see how different methods tend to work out in the long run.

The reward and punishment method

A lot of parents tend to raise their children under the reward and punishment system. Largely this is something that just happens to be the way it is as they aren't really making the definite decision to do so, they just go along with what feels natural. They put on a television show that shows the good guys being good and the bad guys getting in trouble.

They encourage their child to be like the heroes in the movies, and enforce their manner of punishment and praise, hoping that it will all come out in the wash.

If a child misbehaves, they get put in time out. If a child is good, they get treats. It seems pretty straight forward and simple.

Unfortunately, scientific studies have revealed that this isn't enough. Children that grow up under this manner of discipline tend to base their moral choices on the chances of them getting caught in the act.

For example, if there was a $100 bill sitting on the counter of a store with no one around, they would be very likely to take it. However, if, in the same situation, there happened to be a visible camera or someone else in the store, they would then leave the money alone.

Another secondary issue that crops up with this method of raising a child is that they

tend to cling to their 'cyber parents' more than they do their actual guardians.

We all have our childhood heroes, but if those heroes are the ones that did most of the raising, then those are the ones a child is going to turn to when they need to know something.

If a parent is too busy to spend time with their child and instead always puts them in front of the television, what is going to happen when the child wants to learn about other things? Their whole life they learn by watching the internet or the television, and sadly, the internet and the television both can teach violence as much as anything else.

If you were to get online and internet search "how to bully another person", you would be directed to videos that show you exactly how to get that done. This is what children are watching, and this is what they are picking up. If they learn everything from the television, they are going to turn to the television to learn everything.

Another common method of raising children is that parents try to guide them to embrace morality.

The hope behind this method is that children will consider honesty and trustworthiness to be better than violence or lying "just because it is". There isn't anything to enforce *why,* which often leads them to choose the wrong path.

The reason why this isn't effective is because we are all different, and what values we choose to hold may not be the same as the values another person chooses to hang on to.

Consider this:

A hit man was interviewed by a doctor after he went on a killing spree. The hit man proudly announced to the doctor he had killed 30 people, and there was no sign of remorse in the man as he admitted this.

The doctor, surprised, asked if the hit man had also raped the people he had killed.

Offended, the hitman answered, "Of course not! How dare you suggest such a thing?"

To which the doctor replied, "Well, why not?"

"Because I have values" was the reply.

You can see from this example right here, values aren't enough.

How can we apply this to what we know about serial killers and other criminal offenders?

Values and morals as society teaches them and embraces them are only as effective as the individual who embraces them. As you can see in that example, the doctor (and I think it's safe to say the world as a whole) took the point of view that murder and rape are both horrific.

The criminal, on the other hand, held that rape was a terrible and sinister crime, but murder was not. So, he wasn't about to sexually assault anyone, but he wouldn't hesitate to commit murder.

Now, we in society as a whole would be horrified and lock him in prison for his actions, but by his own moral integrity, he doesn't see that he did anything wrong. So can we then blame his parents and teachers for not disciplining him properly?

Can we say that if he were to have received more instruction as a child and been given a more strict way of life that he would then have not turned into a murderer?

Absolutely not.

Parents, teachers, and guardians can only do so much to instill in a child a sense of morality, and at the end of the day, it comes down to what the child does with the information they are taught.

You can sit a child in a classroom and tell them all day long that stealing candy is wrong, giving them examples and graphs and showing them slides on why they shouldn't do it. But, unless they are to decide for themselves that stealing candy is wrong, then they are going to take candy out of the treat jar when no one is looking as soon as they get the chance.

What can we take away from this information?

It's a balance. I am not going to tell you that we should quit with the discipline of our children, or that we should discipline differently. I think that each child needs to grow up under a loving family with instruction and right and wrong at its core.

However, we can dismiss from our minds that lack of discipline (or too much discipline) is the issue. Yes, broken homes are more responsible for generating criminal behavior than loving homes, but there are always exceptions. There are a lot of children that grow up abused and come out of it as normal human beings, and there are cases of children that grew up in loving homes that turned out to be horrendous criminals.

We can definitely say that discipline and the home life plays a part, but I am not going to say that is where it ends. The underlying issue of a serial killer is far deeper than that, and to find it, we have to look inside.

Chapter 4 – Get With the Program

With all of this in mind, let's take a second now to look within.

We all were raised in a specific manner. The person or people that took care of us in our youth had a system by which they lived and raised us how they felt was right. Odds are, they intended to turn out into society functioning members that would do good and not evil to those around them.

Even in homes that are broken, there is still a sense of morality. Be it twisted, even abusive parents are raising children in a certain way to turn them out as adults in a certain way. Now, I am not condoning their abuse in any way, shape, or form, I just don't want you to assume that these killers or serial killers as a whole are left to figure out life for themselves.

They do have a model to follow, and they do have their own sense of right and wrong.

We can focus on the abusive parents, but that will only make our opinions biased and cause us to push the blame in places it doesn't belong. Instead, let's look at the parents that love and discipline their children in hopes they are going to turn out to be great, functioning members of society.

Yet, in spite of all of the best efforts, there is still a lot of crime in the world today. I wish we could point the finger and say that all of the adults that are out there committing these crimes had terrible childhoods, but I can't.

While in the second chapter of this book we did see that broken homes play a large role in the development of a serial killer, there is always the exception.

As I have said before, the fact of the matter is that many of these criminals came out of loving and nurturing homes, and there are countless people that grew up in a loveless home, yet became very normal adults.

I firmly believe there is more to the story than meets the eye. There is more going on inside their brain than a resentment for the people who raised them. Or the people who picked on them. As humans, we are designed to have certain traits born into us... things that are hard to go against by sheer nature.

We are designed to have a horror for gore and disfigurement of other humans, and we are designed to have a disgust for murder and torture. Yet, in the case of serial killers, we see them kill again and again. And in addition to their killing, they kill in brutal and disfiguring ways.

Not that a swift and merciful killing would be excusable by any means, but the fact that they take what they do even further than murder itself shows that there has got to be something else in their brain. Something that either drives them or allows them to act as they do and to commit the crimes they commit.

So let's examine the source of the matter: the human brain.

No matter what the external circumstances are, your brain is responsible for how the information is processed, and controlling what your reaction is going to be to the situation. Sure, other factors may come into play to alter or steer this reaction process, but the final decision made and the course of action taken comes from the brain alone.

The brain is an incredible organ. It only weighs 3 pounds, yet it has complete control over a person. From the function of their body to their wants and desires and emotions to carrying out any action that the person commits.

The brain is equally responsible for us feeling love as feeling hate. Happiness or sadness, joy or suffering. The same brain that plans a project to bring life to many, could also plan a project for the destruction of many. There is no end to the way the brain already surprises us, and to imagine its potential is simply mind boggling.

Scientists have found that there is a very thin line in the brain between mental health and mental illness, and that there are very specific health issues that lead to very specific illnesses.

For example:

Sadness leads to depression.

Fear leads to phobia.

Joy leads to mania.

Aggression leads to violence.

Can you see a pattern here?

It's entirely normal to feel sad, but if you allow these emotions to get out of hand, it is going to turn into depression. The same goes for the other emotions, but aggression seems to be exceptionally strong.

What scientists and doctors alike are currently studying and trying to figure out is how this transition happens.

For yet another example:

Most people dislike spiders. The sight of one crawling on the wall at night is enough to make many people opt for sleeping in the other room, and we laugh at how many people overreact when they have a run in with one of those eight-legged foes.

But this is natural fear. They are still able to live life completely normally. They can go into caves, attics, basements, gardens... anywhere there could potentially be a spider. While they don't enjoy an interaction with one should they find it, they don't alter their life out of fear they are going to find a spider.

A phobic person, on the other hand, is going to take their fear to the extreme. They literally have physical reactions when they see spiders, such as panic attacks, paling, heavy breathing, sweating, and an all-around state of distress. They avoid any and all situations in which they could potentially run into a spider, and if they ever do, the reaction is severe and overwhelming.

What we don't understand, however, is what causes the brain to go from a simple fear to an extreme phobia. Usually it is caused by trauma in relation to the being that the person develops a phobia for, but this isn't always the case.

It is also interesting to note that phobias/ depression/violence are the three mental states that tend to get out of hand quickly. Ironic since they are all negative, and dangerous as aggression tends to be the mental state that is most commonly acted on.

Aggression has been around since the dawn of time. It was put into us to help us survive as a race, but for some, it gets out of hand.

Think about it, if an animal were to have a territory, but no way to protect itself (aggression) it wouldn't take long before it was forced out by another creature. This would repeat itself over and over until the animal had nowhere else to go, and they would become extinct.

With that in mind, aggression in and of itself is not a bad trait. We see it in our own human race, but we call it different things to give it a less primitive sound, and make it more socially acceptable.

You will hear someone say that they are just defending what is their own, or they are standing up for themselves. Or they aren't a doormat, or that they aren't going to let others push them around. You will notice in society that it is those that don't have these kind of guts that are the ones who are taken advantage of, and if society wasn't placed in check with morals and laws, we, too, could force extinction on each other.

With that potential in place for all of humanity as well as extinction in the animal kingdom, aggression has to be a necessary part of life. But when aggression crosses to violence, a problem is created. You see, violence is aggression with the intent to hurt someone else, whether it be physically, emotionally, or otherwise.

Example:

Think of two people out on a date. They go to enjoy a couple of drinks at a bar, and the man gets up to use the restroom. In his absence, another man comes in and starts to make advances on the girl. Nothing showy, just subtle advances like buying her a drink and telling her she's attractive.

Her date comes out of the restroom, sees what is going on, and politely, yet firmly, lets the other man know that she is his date, and therefore he needs to move along. More times than not, this is enough to send the other man on his way. It is a tame form of aggression that is socially acceptable. The man stood up for his date, metaphorically pushing the other man along and out of the picture.

Now, let's consider the same exact situation again. The couple are on their date, the man gets up to use the restroom, and the other man moves in. He is equally subtle as in the first scenario, making the exact same gestures as before. Her date returns from the bathroom, sees the situation, and goes into a frenzy.

He may attack the other man, striking him with his fists. He screams, he throws things. He raises an entire scene that is far from polite or acceptable. He may extend his anger toward the girl and anyone else that is in the room, whether they are involved or not.

This second situation is what describes an act of violence. It is not socially acceptable. It is very harmful, and it never ends in anything good.

But, just as aggression and violence are born into each of us, so are the cues and methods to alleviate it.

In the animal kingdom, when two animals are fighting and one gets the upper hand in the battle, the other will often do something that shows the winning animal that they have given up. For many animals, this is releasing a bit of urine. When the winning animal sees that, they will often break off the attack and it is done and over with.

Now, in the human world, you can't do the same thing to alleviate aggression. If someone is being robbed, and the victim wets their pants, it is unlikely to stop the assailant from taking what they came to take.

So that begs the question, is there something you can do that will cause an assailant to change their minds? If so, what is it, and why does it work?

For the standard criminal, you are better able to appeal to their compassionate side, and it is always worth a shot if you are in that kind of situation

Let's back it up a minute, and differentiate between the two kinds of criminals. If you were to suddenly be kidnapped, and you noticed that the person kidnapping you is nervous, loud, jittery, paranoid, or anything along those lines, you can probably assume he is not a serial killer.

Now, this may not mean that you are in any less danger at that particular moment, as any armed and dangerous criminal is just that: an armed and dangerous criminal but if you were to find yourself at the hands of such a person, there is a definite trick you should try.

Ask for things. Talk about your likes and dislikes. Talk about your needs and the fact that you are loved by a family and you have a family that you love. Mention your name and refuse to be called anything but a respectful term. By doing this, you are enforcing the fact that you are human, and your assailant is going to have to wrestle with the right and wrong of what they are doing.

You can, of course, try the same things if you are in this situation whether you suspect your captor to be a serial killer or not, but you have to remember that serial killers don't feel as other criminals do. They act out of sheer will, with no emotion of any kind behind it.

Of course, you should definitely do what you can to get away, but for the sake of this example, you would definitely have an easier time with the criminal. The reason for this being that they don't necessarily want to harm another human being, and by reminding them that you are one, they have to face the facts of what they are doing.

This is a technique that is known as making yourself human to your captors, and it is taught in a wide variety of arenas because it is effective. Now, a serial killer may or may not react to this method in a favorable way. They are so much alike, yet so different at the same time, it is hard to predict accurately what the next move will be.

And, there is a very specific reason for this.

Serial killers and violent people react to things differently than non-criminals do.

Doctors have run a number of studies on the brains of these people, and what they have found is simply amazing.

In one study, a number of violent offenders were given a series of pictures. These were pictures that were designed to stimulate different parts of the brain, and illicit a different response from the person when viewed.

There were normal pictures... dogs, cats, a chair, a house... nothing out of the ordinary. There were pictures that were supposed to bring happiness. Smiles, flowers, butterflies, clear skies, and a few other things were present. Then there were photos that were to stir up disgust or fear. These were pictures of mutilated bodies, injuries, death, and agony.

The common response in the brain for most people is the same. They are happy when they see the happy pics, they are horrified when they see the others. Doctors are able to track what part of the brain is stimulated and therefore what the reaction is by looking at a screen. When different parts of your brain are active, these computers are able to pick up on that activity and trace the response the brain is having.

The screen has a diagram of the brain pictured on it, the specific brain of the patient that is in the scanner at that moment, and they are able to see what the person is feeling based on what part of the brain is lit up on the screen. It has been a long process to get this to happen, but now that they are able to test different people in this way, they are able to see things in the brain that we only imagined before.

This brings a lot of help to the study when patients are viewing and reacting to pictures. Doctors could see and track with great accuracy what each patient was feeling and when. What was interesting, however, was that in the brains of serial killers, there was no difference.

No matter what they were viewing, they had no change in the way their brain was projected on the screen. The same part of the brain was lit up for an entire variety of pictures, on opposite ends of the graph, too. They had the same reaction to the mutilated bodies that they had to the house and the smiles.

By this study, doctors were able to determine a singular, yet groundbreaking factor: serial killers aren't feeling anything at all when they see these images.

It has long been a belief that serial killers love to kill. Like they get some twisted sort of satisfaction out of killing their victims, and only want to kill for the sheer sake of killing. But due to this study, we have seen both one door open and another door close.

If serial killers don't feel anything when they see these photos, then they must not be feeling anything when they are committing the crimes. If this is the case, then it explains why they are able to do it with such ease and repetition, but what it doesn't explain is why they continue to do it. After all, if you don't feel anything when you do something, why go make the effort to do it, especially when they have everything at stake?

Before we get into the answer of that question, let's first take a look at what is really going on inside of their heads, and why.

The main thing doctors noticed in the reaction of the killers to the test was that they showed no level of fear.

While there weren't necessarily pictures meant to scare the viewer, fear is mixed in with other negative emotions we feel when we see gruesome and grisly images. In the case of the serial killers, there was no fear response whatsoever. The fear response in their brains wasn't activated by the same things it is in the brain of a normal person.

The part of the brain that is responsible for fear, the amygdala, floods with light under a scanner when the person is feeling fear. When the serial killers were tested, however, there was hardly any fear response in their brains at all.

With this in view, doctors wondered if they were just a kind of person that had no fear in their lives, and took that lack of fear to an extreme and preyed upon other people as a result. But, upon further study, they came to discover that there was very little communication taking place in the brain at all.

In a normal human brain, there is a lot of connection between an emotion and an action. We feel something, so we do something. This can be as simple or as intricate as we want it to be.

If we are hungry, we eat something. If we are cold, we turn on the heater, if we fall in love, we get to know that person even more, and eventually marry them. All of these things are examples of how feelings lead to actions. That is the way it works.

But for serial killers, there was no connection between what they were doing and how they felt. Through the interviews we have had with serial killers of all kinds, we have found this to be true in many different areas of their lives. They would feel something of an attachment to a person, so they would marry, but they never actually felt love.

They would be attracted to their partner, so they would engage in intimacy, but they weren't driven by love, or feel any greater connection to their partner after they were intimate. They would walk the streets and see all kinds of things, but they wouldn't have a response to it.

They could commit the most horrendous crime of all, and not feel a thing while they were doing it, or after.

This is because the frontal lobe of the brain is damaged. It hasn't formed correctly, and the life the criminal lived up to that point was all just adding fuel to the fire.

This is no excuse, but it does help you understand better the why behind the method. Of course there is no reason for them to do what they do, but if you realize they don't feel anything, and they have the mindset of violence, they are only acting as they see fit.

Think of it this way: if you were to take a lion, and put him in the middle of New York City, he would attack people. He would injure and kill, and probably do as much damage as he could, but he wouldn't feel any remorse for it or any other emotion for that matter. He is a lion and a lion is going to do what a lion does without any real thought to it before or after what he has done.

The same goes for serial killers. Not that they are animals or are acting out of fear, but rather they don't think what they are doing is wrong, so they do it freely, not worrying about how they feel about it.

While for most of us, this is hard to fathom and we can't really wrap our minds around what is going on inside of their heads, knowing that they aren't thinking the same as everyone else does help you understand them a bit better.

But if this is true, then why do they seek to hide what they have done? There are a lot of serial killers out there that go for years undiscovered because they have committed these crimes, then covered them up so well that no one ever suspected them.

I know it doesn't make sense to a point, but hear me out, and you will understand why they choose to hide what they are doing. First of all, there are a lot of people that say if you are hiding something, then you know it is wrong, but that isn't always true.

You can do something that you think is right, but hide it because others feel that it is wrong and you don't want to get in trouble for it.

Still don't believe me? Hold on, and you will.

Marijuana. Marijuana is a very widely smoked substance in our day and age. If you watch the news at all, you are aware that there has been an ongoing battle on whether or not it should be legalized. If you have been watching the news, you also know that right now it is illegal in most states, and that there is a pretty steep fine as well as potential jail time for the use of it outside of medicinal purposes.

Now, you are probably also aware that there are a lot of people who recreationally smoke this substance in their free time. They don't think it's wrong, they think that it's good, and they think it ought to be legal, but if a policeman were to come around, they would hide it in a heartbeat, and destroy any evidence that they had anything to do with it.

So by this example, would you say that they know they are wrong for smoking marijuana, or would you say they just don't want to get in trouble for it? If you went with the second option, I would have to agree with you.

There are countless people across the globe that regularly engage in activities that they don't think is wrong, they just know that most people feel that it's wrong, and they fear getting in trouble if people know that they are doing it.

Yes, it is an extreme form of this mindset, but that is the same way a lot of serial killers think about the crimes they commit.

But there are a lot of people who would smoke pot if it were made legal but don't do it now because they don't want to get caught. By this line of thinking, are there potential serial killers out there that just don't do anything because they are scared they will get caught?

As unnerving as it is, there are. Just because the serial killers that are caught don't have any emotions in their brain, it doesn't mean that there aren't people out there that are somewhere in the middle.

The murderous mindset is the result of the combination of several factors. With that in mind, if one of the factors wasn't present, then there could potentially be people out there that would be serial killers if they thought they could get away with it.

That is where the study of this mindset also comes into play. While we can't go around and accuse people of things they might do if they thought they could get away with it, what we can do is study how these people are working, and look for the signs that manifest themselves early on. If we do this, we can also take other measures to steer them away from the path that molds them into the killers they are.

It's hard to know exactly when they cross over from only thinking about doing something to actually committing it, but once that happens, it only gets worse. It is rare to see someone that is on that path turn around before anything bad happens, but hopefully, if we are better able to see the signs and prevent it in the first place, we can cut back on the number of deaths that could happen in the future.

Chapter 5 – The Trigger Factor

Let's take a turn now to the beginning. Let's look at what causes these things to form inside of the mind of a killer as a child, and what it is that causes them to take the direction they take. As we have said before, we all start in the same way, so there are other things that have to come into play that mold these people into the killers they end up being.

So where does it all begin? What makes these killers tick? And what sets off that clock?

To better understand it, let's again make it personal. After all, as dangerous as these people are, they are people, too, and they do have the same basic frame of mind that the rest of us do.

The ugly truth of the trigger factor

No matter what you are struggling with in life, there is a trigger that sets you off. Even if you don't consider it to be a struggle, the thing that you like to do the most is often set off by some sort of action. This can be something blatant such as antagonizing, or it may be a lot more subtle. So subtle, in fact, you may not even know what it is.

If you are naturally inclined to do something, it doesn't really matter what the trigger is, the action that you use as a response is going to be your reaction no matter what.

For example, if you were to have an issue with emotional eating, you are going to turn to eating for any kind of day you were having. If you were to have a good day, you would celebrate with food. If you were to have a bad day, you would make yourself feel better with food.

If you were nervous, food would be your distraction. See the pattern? Your trigger is completely different, but the action is the same. You get the promotion at work you have been dreaming about, here comes the ice cream. You got fired from your job unfairly and unexpectedly, here comes the same ice cream.

You don't know when it started. For as long as you can remember you turned to food to make yourself feel a certain way. You don't ever remember making the decision that food was going to be your go to, but you do remember choosing it.

Food is completely harmless in and of itself, but violence is not, and violent people are the same way. They may get scared, and fight. They may get happy, and be too rough. They may be mad, and take out their anger in a very violent way.

These people don't remember when they decided that violence was the answer to their problems, but it is something that they have been doing for as long as they can remember, and with that being the case, they feel that violence really is the answer to anything that is happening in their lives.

Most violent offenders start young. This has been fairly well-known in the past, but it is becoming increasingly alarming.

Usually the signs start on the playground. It's not the fun kind of teasing you see pass back and forth between friends, it is downright bullying. This may be verbal or physical, depending on the situation, but it does grow worse from there.

There have been reports given by the classmates of famous serial killers that as a child, the criminal was always pushing them around. Depending on the particular situation, there are grown serial killers that would pull knives on their classmates at school, would make fun of them and abuse them, and may have even attacked them more than once.

There was a serial killer in Germany that killed a girl that went to his school when he was 16 and she was 18. He was turned free, wiped clean of his guilt because he had committed the act when he was a minor. He went on to kill at least 36 more people.

The famous serial killer Ted Bundy killed numerous girls on the campus he lived on, and he was close to their age. Another killer murdered 6 of his classmates when they were seniors in college, and hid the evidence so well that he wasn't found guilty of the murders until he personally brought up the fact that he had done it when he was being tried for a different series of murders decades later.

Is it really curiosity that killed the cat?

Another common sign of a child that is going to grow up to be violent is cruelty to animals. More than one serial killer is said to have mutilated, abused, tortured, and killed animals when they were a child. Some tortured, then did horrible things to the animal such as burying them alive, only to dig them up again later on and torture them some more.

Others have taken baseball bats to animals, knives, rocks, and all other horribly forms of cruelty. They may kill the animal, they may torture it so much that it dies later on of its wounds, or they may abuse it and turn it free. Violence in one way or another... even brutal killing isn't uncommon.

This is largely because they are getting a feel for it. They may or may not be sure about what they want to do, and animals are a good way to experience the action without having a lot of consequence. More than one serial killer to be said that they started on animals, simply because they were curios of what it would be like to kill another creature. The same statement has been said by more than one serial killer that murdered their classmates.

They were "curious".

But keep in mind that cruelty to animals is just the next step. It gets worse and worse until they finally move on to human victims for good.

Example 1

A little boy likes to push around the kids in his class. He does so in a seemingly innocent manner at first, but it grows. By the time he reaches middle school he has moved on to wounding or killing pigeons with rocks or other items he finds. Then it turns to domestic animals.

By the time he's in high school, he's in fights and detention all the time. After graduation, the domestic violence starts. And it continues to get worse from there.

As interesting as it is, serial killers have both a lot in common and not much in common at the same time. For many, however, there is a common thread in their victims. You will notice that they only attack young women. Or they only attack a certain race.

Perhaps it's a certain hair color, age, gender, ethnicity combined. Whatever the case may be, you don't often see a serial killer with a wide range of victims. They might have a lot of victims, but there is always something these victims have in common.

Example 2

Sometimes, a serial killer chooses their victims based on a person or persons that caused them harm when they were young. Jeffery Dahmer was abused by his father as a child, and he grew up to become a rapist and a murderer of men.

And while most serial killers are men, there are still their female counterparts. We don't know for sure why female serial killers are so far less than men, although there are the speculations, but consider this female serial killer that is still in prison to this day.

She is in prison for murdering 18 elderly women. She would murder them by strangling them with her stocking or a rope, tying knots around their necks. There wasn't much these women had in common. They didn't work the same kind of jobs, they didn't drive the same kind of cars, they didn't live in the same part of town.

They were from all over... but she hunted them down, pretended to be their friend, and waited for her moment to strike.

Now, you would probably wonder who, even in their craziest of states would prey upon old women as their victims. Usually we think of the horror movie stereotype of a pretty young woman or a good looking young man, not an old lady that has no way to defend herself and wouldn't dream of harming a fly.

But these women were the exact target that our serial killer here was looking for.

When interviewed, she was asked why she specifically killed only elderly women. After all, there are a lot of people out there, and many of them would be just as vulnerable as the women she was preying on.

The answer, though horrifying, wasn't at all surprising.

As it turned out, this serial killer's own mother had verbally abused her when she was a child. If she did poorly in school, she was beaten and called all kinds of horrible things.

If she did well in school, she wouldn't receive anything better. Through the years, she grew more and more angry with her mother, and became so bitter she didn't have many real friends.

As an adult, she harbored a deep seeded hatred for her mother, and felt like she murdered her mother with each woman she killed. Of course, this is no excuse for the crimes, but you can see that there was definitely a trigger point for her.

She didn't necessarily think of killing each of the women as individual women with their own lives and families. She would picture her mother in each one of them, and with the murder of each one of them, would try to alleviate the hatred she felt inside of her every time she thought of her mother.

But, you think, *experimentally harming animals and taking your anger on your mother out on innocent women doesn't justify turning into a full blown serial killer.*

Surely there are lots of people with pent up anger or no empathy that don't turn into these killers we see on the news.

That's correct. There is more to it than just wanting to get anger out or to not have a care for another living thing. After all, there really are a lot of these people out there that don't do any harm to society.

The fact is these serial killers have something else in common that is much deeper than just common interest. There is an actual development issue in their brain that many scientists and researchers believe to be the cause of their aggression. Now, there are a number of factors that come into play that cause this to happen to these people, but it is true that there is something wrong with their brains.

Although there is that lack of empathy on their side, it is rare for a killer to start with humans. They usually start small or in a different way than build up to something bigger.

As you saw in the last chapter, they don't have the same response to fear or joy or any other emotion as most people do, but rather, they lack that connection between what is going on and how they feel about it. This is what turns them into functioning human beings, but unfeeling human beings.

When this goes on long enough, they start to take their aggression out on the world around them. It is just a matter of time.

Chapter 6 – Is the Gene Pool to Blame?

All too often, when we see a behavior being carried out in a person, we blame the family. It must be in their blood. It must be something in them that isn't in other people that causes them to act that way or commit that crime.

While we know that violent people do have a difference in the way their brain works, we can't necessarily blame that on genes. Genes are things that are passed on from person to person, but if that were the case here, there should be entire families of serial killers.

But, if you were to look into the background of any of the serial killers you can think of, they are the only child in the family they grew up in to become a serial killer as an adult. In the rare case, you can see two people who are married or dating turn into killers together, but you don't see families in which the entire group are killers.

You can argue that in certain families, there are really bad things that go on, but I counter argue that most serial killers had siblings, and they are the only ones that grew up to kill. For example, Fred West grew up in a family of many children. They were all sexually abused by their father and mother.

They were all put under the same treatment, and they were all under the same set of rules, but it is only Fred that came out of that family a killer. His wife, Rose, grew up under similar circumstances, but she, too, had another sister.

They were both abused, they were both taken from their father, and yet Rose is the only one to grow up to be a killer. If it were in the genes of the family, then in both families both all of the children should have grown to be killers, as well as their parents, grandparents, and their own children.

Genes in and of themselves do not produce violence. Violence is brought out in a person based on a lot of different factors.

Genes in and of themselves are the blue prints of our personalities. We get a lot of our looks, behaviors, and tendencies from our genes, but we don't have to follow them. This is why you will see parents and children that are completely opposite.

There is, however, a gene inside many people that is known as the violence gene. It is officially known as the MAOA, and it can potentially cause a lot of aggression in the person who has it. While the person is in control of their own action, they do have to battle a greater influence within themselves than those that don't have this gene.

On the other hand, there are a lot of people out there with this gene that are not aggressive. There are, in fact, a number of other variables that come into play, too, which makes serial killers act the way they do.

Think of a person that you know that is easily pushed to tears. It doesn't take a lot, and they are bawling their head off. The reason this is happening is because of a hormone that is inside of them. You may know a person that used to be that way, and now isn't, or you may know a person that wasn't always that way, and now is.

It all depends on how they are choosing to act. Yes, there are things that are inside all of us naturally. Tendencies and feelings, ideas and struggles, but at the end of the day, what we do is our own choice. No one and nothing is making us do any of it besides ourselves and our own choices.

An interesting thing to take note of, however, is that this is a gene that is primarily passed down to children through their mother. This is why men are more often psychopathic serial killers than women. They get the gene from their mother alone, which gives it more prominence in their life. A daughter, on the other hand, gets an x gene from her mother and an x gene from her father, which sort of dilutes the issue in her.

So while not impossible, it is unlikely that a woman is going to turn into a serial killer as much as a man would.

The other factors that come into play that largely cause people with the MAOA gene to reach their breaking point is an imbalance in the brain, a chemical imbalance, and a traumatic event in their childhood.

As we saw in chapter 3, there is a lot of differences in the development of the brain of a serial killer versus the brain of someone undergoing normal development. Scientists, however, say that there is more to it than just a brain difference.

After all, there are a lot of people out there today with brain differences. Some people experience mental disability, others are harder to get along with, some are just slightly different than what would be considered normal. But none of them are psychotic or have any kind of violent tendencies.

With that in mind, we can take the knowledge that there is an issue with the brain, and combine it with the fact certain people are carriers of a more violent gene. Now, when you combine both of those factors, you have the start of a problem. But even those two alone are not enough to produce a full blown serial killer.

So what are the other two factors?

A chemical imbalance and trauma.

If we back up a little bit and look at the developing baby inside of his mother, we see a child that has a few problems with his brain. If we combine that with the fact his mother passed on to him the MAOA gene, we are in the red zone. Then, if there is the right chemical imbalance during development in the womb (as there sometimes is) you have the third factor.

This is rare, but it does happen. Sometimes, in the womb babies are exposed to too much serotonin. Now, serotonin as the chemical in our brains that is supposed to relax us. When it is released in our brains, we feel at peace, and like we can handle the situation.

If a baby is exposed to too much of this from the beginning, they have a greater tolerance to the chemical, and as a result they are almost numb to the effects of the chemical in their brain when it is released later on in life. This means that they can't ever really feel that calming peace.

They really don't feel anything at all. It is just an emptiness that they have to deal with, and they do deal with through acting out.

But even these three factors alone aren't enough to produce the serial killer we're talking about. There is that final factor, one that is sadly all too common in the day in which we live.

A traumatic event

I'm not talking about mild stress that goes along in any child's life, I mean a full blown act of trauma that imbeds in them a feeling of hate and despair, and basically pushes them over the edge. This can be something like a car accident, a fire, physical abuse by a loved one or someone else, or just a society of violence. The more they are exposed to it, the more normal it seems to be.

This is why we need to look at how to break the cycle and introduce a different way of dealing with the feelings they have.

So what does this mean in the big picture?

While genes do play a part in who you are and what you do, they aren't entirely responsible for everything you do. Serial killers are not born that way, although they might have some genetic makeup that could turn them that way.

In truth, all of us have the capability to become a serial killer, or at least we did when we were young, but what steered us away from that direction is how we were treated. Not how we were raised, but how we were treated.

A history of violence is going to produce more violence in an adult's life.

A child that is given everything they want from the moment they are born to when they grow up is going to grow up spoiled. They are going to be demanding, they are going to think they deserve everything, and they are going to view the world as revolving around them.

If they are raised treated well, they are only going to end up spoiled. The same goes for someone that grew up poor. They may feel like they don't deserve anything better, or that they have their lot in life, but they aren't going to take a turn of violence if they were raised in love.

Yet the children that endured abuse, physical or mental, are the ones that grow up to have greater issues. They turn to violence as the answer to everything and anything... largely because violence is the only thing they know.

Chapter 7 – Prevention and a Hope for the Future

Whenever you are able to get a glimpse inside of the mind of a serial killer, or any other violent criminal, what you see makes you want to shudder. There is a lot of darkness inside of a person that has no emotion, and to think of what they are capable of is enough to give you nightmares for weeks.

But there is good news. We don't have to leave the situation at that. There is a way we can all contribute to the good of society and ending this trend that has been around for centuries.

The more research we have done on the mind of criminals, the easier it is to see why they do what they do, and from that information gain an understanding on how to stop creating more people like them.

I truly believe based on the studies I have seen that there is an answer to this behavior. So much of what we do as people are either things that we were actively taught to do as children, or things that we picked up on at a certain point given the behavior we saw going on around us.

So that leaves us with the question:

Is there a critical period of time in which intervention could save a child from growing up into a serial killer or violent offender?

If you think about it, we are all born with a blank slate. We have the same pure mind, and the same set of emotions. We are given the same chance to grow and make our own choices, and live life the right way.

With that being said, and with what we have learned about serial killers thus far, it is pretty obvious to think that there must be a time in a child's life when all of this started. It can't have just happened overnight, and odds are there was something prompting the decisions on.

But what were they? Is it during the confusing teen years, or does it happen much earlier?

The answer may surprise you.

At 3 years old, behavioral problems start to show themselves

Behavioral problems may not be anything major. They could be as small as not listening in class or running around when they were supposed to be sitting quietly. As a result, these children spend a lot of time in trouble, and may spend a lot of the day alone in time out.

From there, the problems only get worse, until you have an avalanche of problems that are overbearing when you have to deal with them all at once.

At 5 to 7 years old, learning disorders become evident

By this time, since there were behavior problems in the beginning and they weren't given the attention they needed, they have problems learning how to read and write.

The more problems they have, the more frustration they feel, but sadly, the more time they spend in trouble instead of getting the help they need to succeed. As a result, they continue to slip further and further away from the right path, and make choices towards violence for the answers.

At 11 to 13 years of age, they start to talk about gangs

The isolated behavior makes them feel as though they are alone, which they may prefer, but they are still going to look for those that can relate. This is why they talk about joining gangs, and why those gang members are so much alike.

The reason it works this way is a direct link back to what we looked at before. The brain isn't communicating with itself properly, which means that these children are often functioning without a lot of emotion behind what they are doing. The little emotions they do feel tends to be negative ones, such as aggression, anger, and sadness.

They become trapped in this cycle where they don't care about what is going on around them, except for when it in direct association to them. If something benefits them, they pay attention to it, but if it doesn't, they don't really even acknowledge.

Outside sources can help instill these things in a child if they are consistent and persistent.

Thankfully, this isn't a lost cause. On the outset of this, it would appear as though we are trapped in a world full of people that are going to turn out a certain way, and there is nothing we can do about it, but in reality, there is a lot we can do to help these children, and alter the future that awaits this world as a result.

Family

It is said that problems begin in the home, but I want to counter that with the hope that solutions also begin in the home. While it is true that a lot of children are in bad situations, that doesn't mean there isn't hope.

Poverty has a way of breeding hopelessness in people. It is in the parents, and it stems down to the children. In order to help the kids from ever reaching that first stage, we need to break the cycle of poverty they are facing in their lives. Now, I am not saying that we can end poverty, there are countless numbers that have tried, and unfortunately, that is just something we can't do, but we can break the cycle of poverty.

Teach the parents how to take care of themselves. Hygiene and clothing that fits go a long way, even if you don't spend a lot of money on those items. Children that are raised under a roof in which the family cares for itself and each other are children that turn out better in the long run.

To do this for families, we need to support the groups that are working with these parents and teaching them to break the cycle. To do things that will benefit themselves and their children in the long run. As soon as we can break this cycle in the beginning, we are going to have a head start for school.

School

School systems need to work with the children, and see to it that everyone is learning. If the kids are fulfilled with a sense of purpose, they are going to be less likely to go around picking fights and bullying.

School programs that encourage the children to participate and offer room for growth will do wonders in the secondary fight against this cycle. It is when the kids with the problems are shoved aside either in detention or in time out if they are younger that they stop learning or trying to learn. They need to have an end goal, and work towards that if we want to see them succeed.

Society

Society isn't really something we can head out and fix as it is, but it is something we can fix over time with who we raise. The adults that are in the world right now make their own decisions. They do what they do because they want to do it, but if we can raise our children to grow up and contribute to society, we are going to raise a generation that can change the state we are currently in.

We need to teach our children to have a respect for authority, and how to interact with each other in a respectful manner. The more we ignore the problem and tell kids they don't have to look out for anyone but themselves, the harder it is going to be to break this cycle.

This is going to overflow into how they raise their children, and how the following generations grow.

Are we desensitizing our society and the children in it?

One of the major conflicts of society today is the entertainment industry. We see so much violence taking place on the big screen and in the video games that flood the shelves of our malls that it's harder to find a game that is family friendly than it is to find one that is full of blood and gore.

Now, this is not to say that people who play these games don't have a problem with blood and gore, but if you think about it, and all of the little children that are allowed to play these games, they are growing up in a world in which blood and gore is a form of entertainment.

Not to mention that developers are constantly trying to create games that are more realistic, more violent, and more graphic as time goes by. Sure, they slap on their ratings, but what does that do for parents that don't really know what is going on?

And if you take a single look into the movie industry, you will find that the things we allow to take place on screen in this modern day are so different than the things that were allowed even 10 years ago that it's not even funny. We see nudity, crimes, murder, bloodshed, and swearing all taking place in movies that are rated PG-13.

PG-13 is supposedly ok for children that are only 13 years old. That isn't even in high school yet, and they are going to see murder and other crimes take place in a graphic way? What is that going to do to their developing minds? Sure, the odds of them actually growing up to become like the criminals they see on the movie is slim, but what we are doing is taking away the shock value from them.

If we do this often enough, we create in society a people that isn't shocked or bothered by blood or gore. They see it enough, they play it enough, it looks real enough, that the shock factor is gone. This means that if you were to take them in 10 years and put them under that same test that the serial killers took, the one with the pictures, they aren't going to have any different of a reaction from the blood and gore than the serial killers did.

And that is just downright disturbing.

What does that mean for me right now?

In this book, you have gotten a glimpse at how violent offenders work. They are people, just like you and me, but they are acting on a different level. A level that could potentially cause harm to those around them. It is important to watch for the signs in those around you, and do your part in making society a safe place for the children that are coming after.

I know it's not feasible to go around and prevent children from watching violent shows or playing violent games, but if we all work together, we can make a difference on how much the producers and developers are allowed to get away with in a game or a movie.

If we are consistent enough at this, we can slow down or even stop the level of violence they are involved in through the entertainment industry, and we can get involved in their real life development.

This isn't an issue we can stick our head in the sand about and wish that it didn't exist. We don't have to live life in fear, but we do need to be aware of what is going on, too. If we all work together, we can set up schools that help all children, no matter what their abilities are. No one is going to be pushed aside or left in the corner.

We can work on studies to help women in prenatal care and keep their hormones balanced, not to mention vitamins and minerals that can help babies as they're growing inside their mothers. The more we can work to slow or stop the triggers that turn people into killers, the more we can rid society of the threat.

I hope you are able to take the things I have put into this book and use them for good. We can all make a difference if we try, so don't let anything hold you back from stepping in.

Conclusion

Thank you again for getting this book!

I hope this book was able to help you to see inside the mind of criminals, and learn how they work.

The next step is to continue to study the why's behind the issue, and work to end the criminal activity that takes place in this world we live in. It is really hard to combat when you think of all the people out there that struggle with this very thing, but it is a fact that if we are to catch it early enough, we can make a difference.

Whether you read this book for common knowledge, or if you are studying to enter the field in some way, you can use what you learned here and apply it to what you see when you are out in the world.

Next time you turn on the television and see a news story about a violent crime, dive into it a little bit, take a look at the background and see what was going on behind the scenes if you can. You will be fascinated by what you uncover.

I truly believe that the answer to ending this lies within all of us, we just have to work together to get it out of our children, and eventually out of society. The question is, how are you going to be a part of that change?

Are you going to be the one who doesn't buy that game, or doesn't go to that movie? Are you going to be the one to show that child how to be kind to the creatures around him? Are you going to do your part in making a difference in the world as a whole?

Finally, if you enjoyed this book, then I'd like to ask you for a favor, would you be kind enough to leave a review for this book on Amazon? It'd be greatly appreciated! If you did not like the book I would love to hear what I could do better. Email me at robertforbes@gmail.com.

Go to Amazon and search for this title to leave a review for this book.

Also, make sure to take a look at my other book:

*"**Serial Killers:** The Top 12 Most Evil Serial Killers to Ever Live and the True Stories of Their Crimes"*

You can find it by searching for its title on amazon.

Thank you and good luck!

Made in the USA
San Bernardino, CA
19 June 2019